THE WORLD'S BEST-SELLING GUIDE TO THE MOST USEFUL CHORDS

# THE GUITARIST'S
# Color Picture
# Chords

## NOW IN FULL COLOR

**Wise Publications**
New York/London/Paris/Sydney/Copenhagen/Berlin/Madrid/Toyko

**Music Sales America**

DISTRIBUTED BY

**HAL•LEONARD®**
CORPORATION
7777 W. BLUEMOUND RD. P.O. BOX 13819 MILWAUKEE, WI 53213

Written by Happy Traum.
Book design & layout: Sorcha Armstrong
Cover design by Mike Bell
Photography by Randall Wallace
Chord diagrams by Digital Music Art

Order No. AM974776
ISBN: 978-0-7119-9541-3
This book Copyright © 2003 by Wise Publications.

**Your Guarantee of Quality:**
As publishers, we strive to produce every book to the highest commercial
standards. This book has been carefully designed to minimise awkward
page turns and to make playing from it a real pleasure. Particular care has
been given to specifying acid-free, neutral-sized paper made from pulps
which have not been elemental chlorine bleached. This pulp is from
farmed sustainable forests and was produced with special regard for the
environment. Throughout, the printing and binding have been planned to
ensure a sturdy, attractive publication which should give years of
enjoyment. If your copy fails to meet our high standards, please inform
us and we will gladly replace it.

www.musicsales.com

# contents

# tuning guide

There are several ways of tuning the guitar. If you're playing in a band then the guitar must be tuned to the instrument that cannot be readily tuned, that is, the electric organ, piano or harp. Tuning can be done easily by following the diagram below and tuning each string in turn as shown.

If you're a soloist then it really doesn't make any difference if the notes you play are actual concert notes, as long as each note is tuned in relation to the others on the guitar.

To tune this way, tune the E string (the heaviest one) so that it vibrates easily, does not buzz yet is not too taut. You could also tune the string using an electronic tuner or pitch pipes.

Press down the fifth fret on the bottom E string (the note A). Now play the open A string. Tune the A string by turning the tuning pegs, so that it sounds the same as the fifth fret E string note.

Follow this procedure, tuning each string in turn to the one above it:

• Hold down the fifth fret on the E string and tune to the A string.

• Hold down the fifth fret on the A string and tune to the D string.

• Hold down the fifth fret on the D string and tune to the G string.

• Hold down the fourth fret on the G string and tune to the B string.

• Hold down the fifth fret on the B string and tune to the E string.

You will probably find (especially with new strings) that you need to re-tune often. However, with a little practice, you should find it easier.

## keyboard tuning diagram

## relative tuning diagram

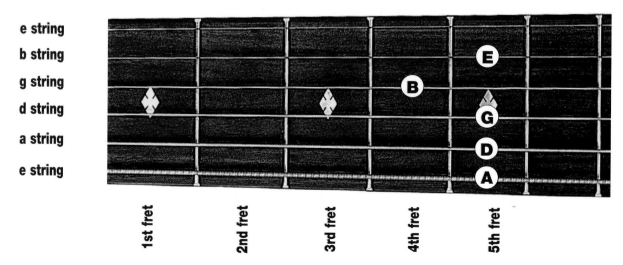

# understanding chord diagrams

The chord diagram is a picture, or map, of the guitar fingerboard. Six vertical lines represent the six strings, and the shorter, horizontal lines represent the frets. Circles indicate the place at which the string is fretted, and the number within the circle indicates the finger of the left hand to be used.

Each diagram is drawn as if the guitar were facing you, in a vertical position. Therefore, the sixth, or bass string, is on the left, and the first, or top string, is on the right.

An **x** next to a string indicates that the string is not picked or strummed by the right hand. It is sometimes necessary to block out, or damp, a string that you do not want to sound. This is done by touching that string lightly, so as to stop it from vibrating. For instance, when playing the A9 chord, your second finger (left hand) can easily touch the fifth string, and your fourth finger can touch the first string, thereby silencing those strings. In chords where the x is on the 6th string, it is better to just strum from the 5th string.

Strings that have an **o** symbol above them are to be played open (i.e. not fretted).

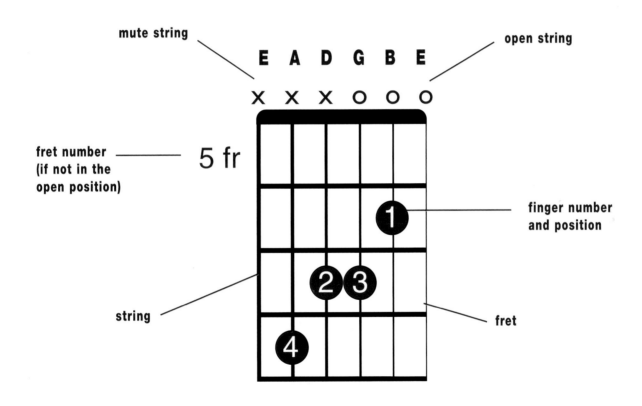

In this book, one photograph is shown for each type of chord, but three diagrams are shown. The first diagram is the most commonly used type. It is also most likely to be an open chord, and therefore easier to play.

The other two shapes shown are alternative voicings to the main chord, usually higher up the neck or as barre chords. These are also known as 'movable' chords, as they can be moved around the neck to produce different chords.

# KEY OF A

### A

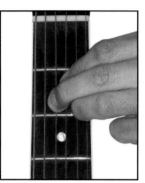
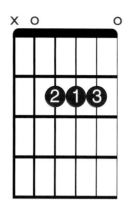
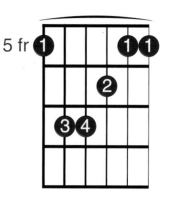
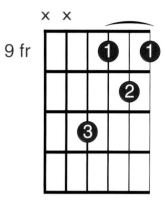

### A7

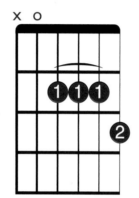
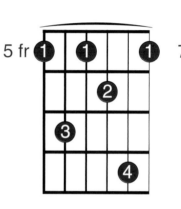
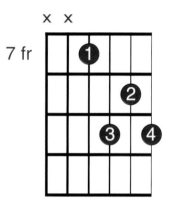

### Am

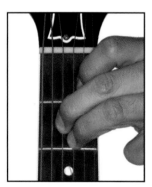
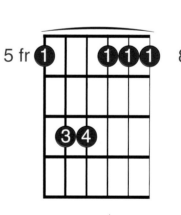
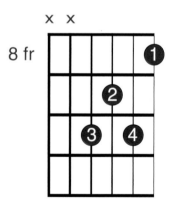

### Am7

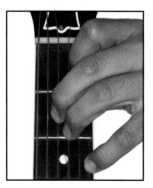
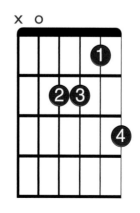
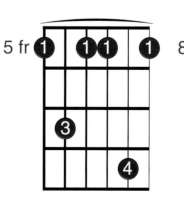
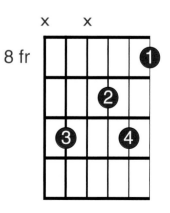

# KEY OF A

**A6**

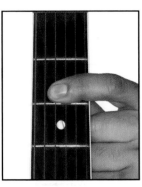
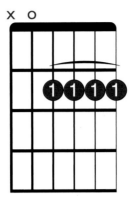
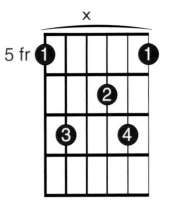
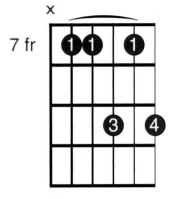

**Am6**

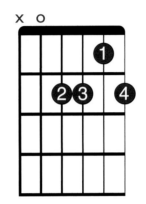
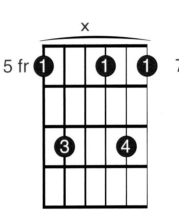
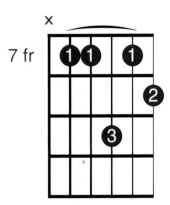

**A maj7**

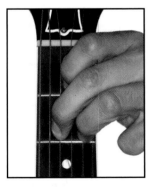
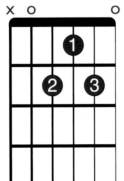
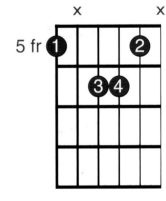

**A9**

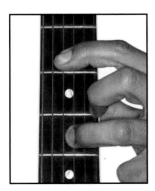
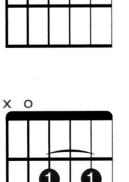
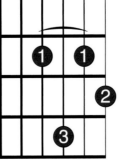
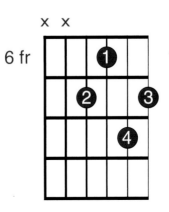
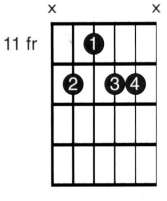

**B♭**

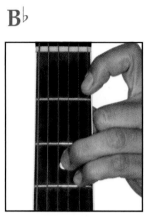
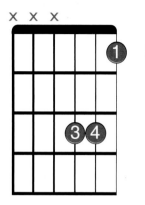

3 fr

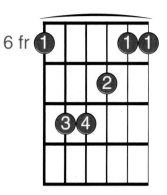

6 fr

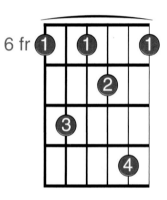

**B♭7**

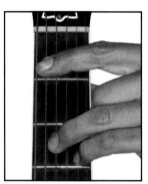
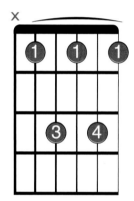
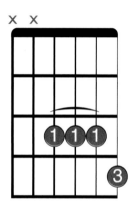

6 fr

**B♭m**

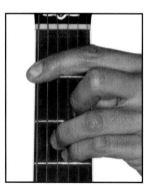
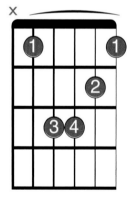

6 fr

9 fr

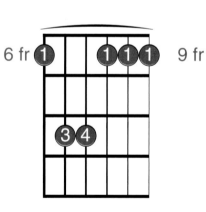

**B♭m7**

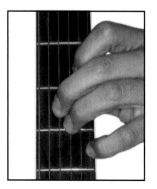
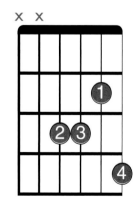

6 fr

9 fr

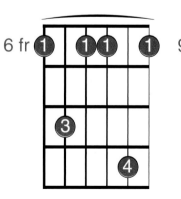
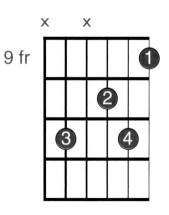

8

### B♭6

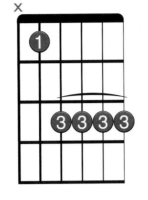

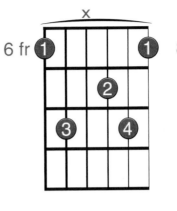

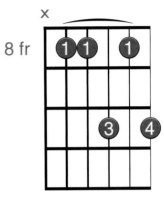

6 fr

8 fr

### B♭m6

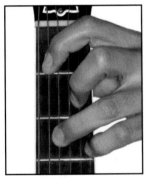

6 fr

8 fr

### B♭ maj7

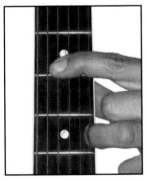

3 fr

5 fr

### B♭9

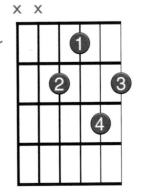

7 fr

8 fr

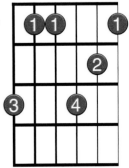

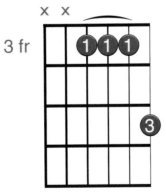

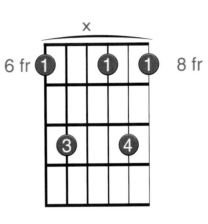

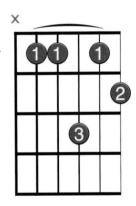

**B**

**B**

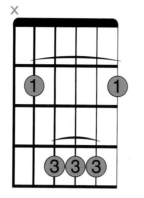
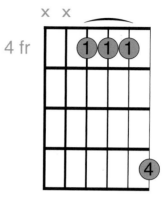
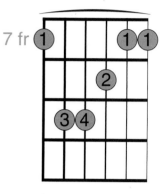

4 fr

7 fr

**B7**

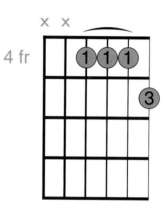
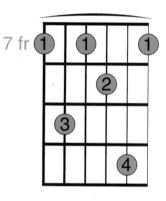

4 fr

7 fr

**Bm**

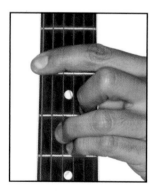
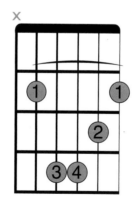
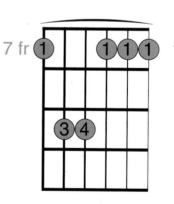
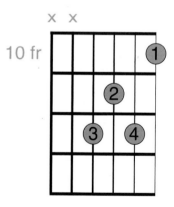

7 fr

10 fr

**Bm7**

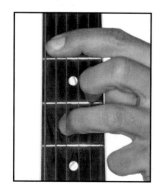
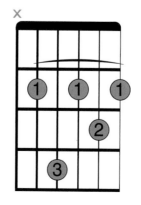
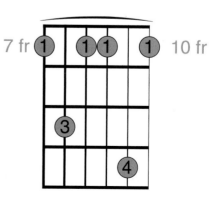
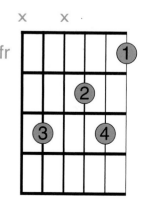

7 fr

10 fr

**B**

## B6

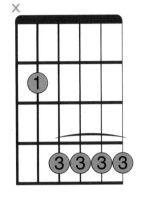

7 fr

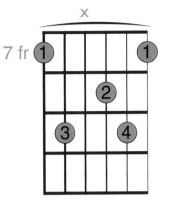

9 fr

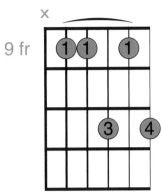

## Bm6

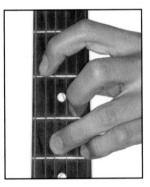

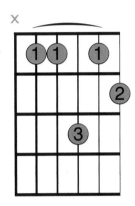

7 fr

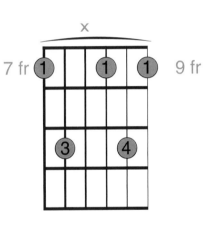

9 fr

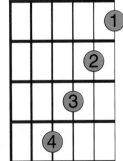

## B maj7

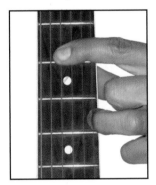

4 fr

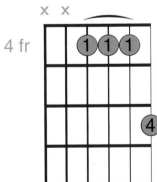

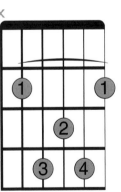

6 fr

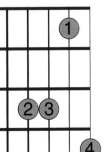

## B9

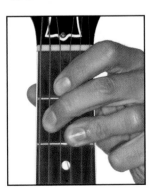

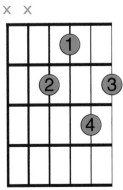

2 fr

8 fr

## C

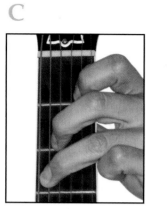
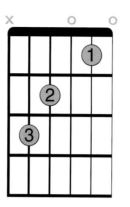
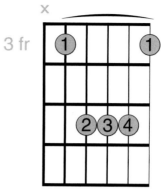
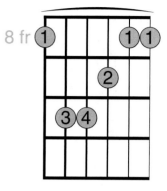

3 fr

8 fr

## C7

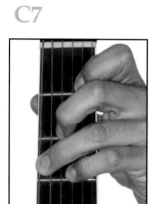
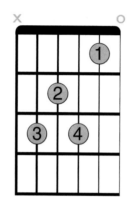
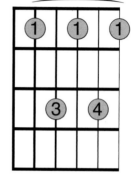
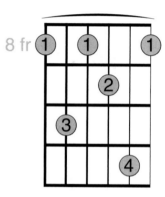

3 fr

8 fr

## Cm

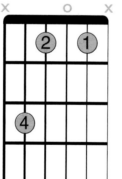
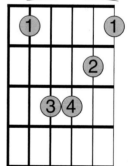
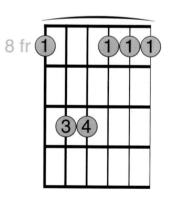

3 fr

8 fr

## Cm7

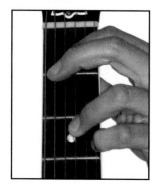
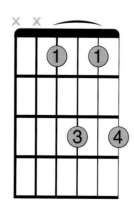
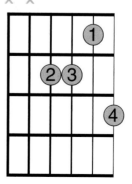
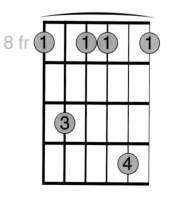

4 fr

8 fr

## C6

## Cm6

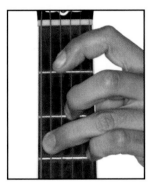

## C maj7

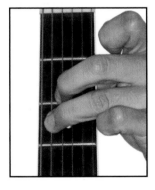

## C9

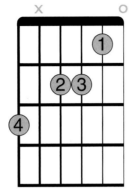

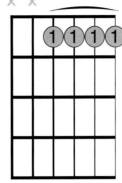

5 fr

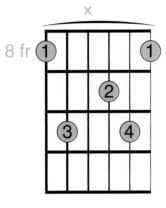

8 fr

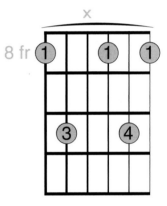

4 fr

8 fr

3 fr

7 fr

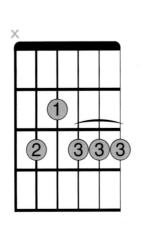

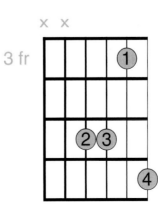

3 fr

9 fr

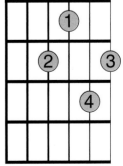

## C#

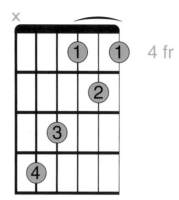

4 fr

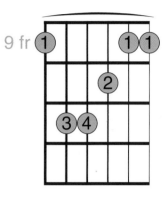

9 fr

## C#7

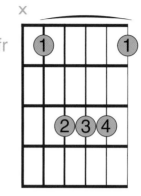

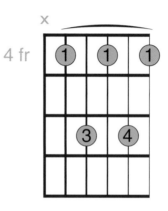

4 fr

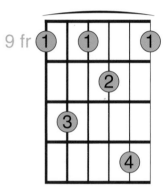

9 fr

## C#m

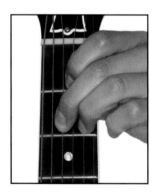

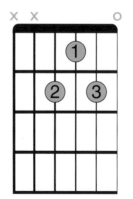

4 fr

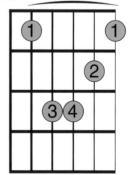

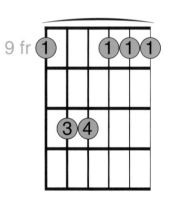

9 fr

## C#m7

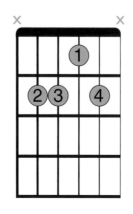

5 fr

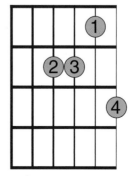

9 fr

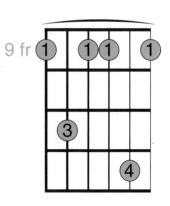

**C#6**

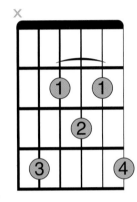

6 fr

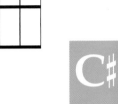

9 fr

**C#m6**

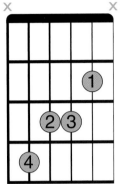

5 fr

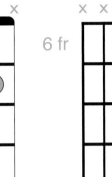

9 fr

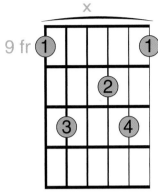

**C# maj7**

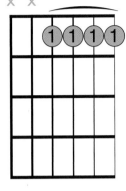

4 fr

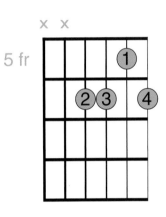

8 fr

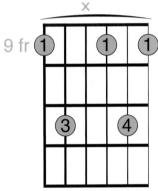

**C#9**

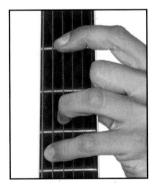

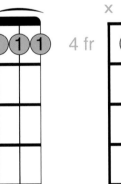

4 fr

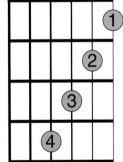

10 fr

C#

**C#9**

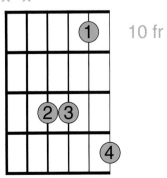

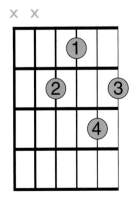

# KEY OF D

## D

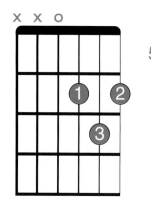
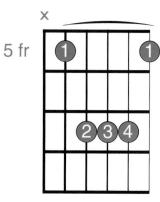
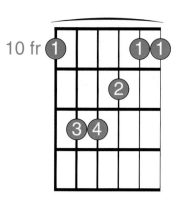

## D7

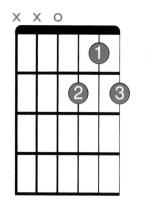
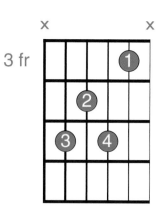
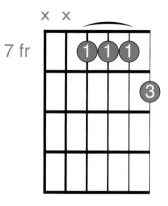

## Dm

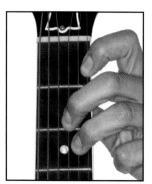
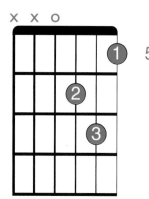
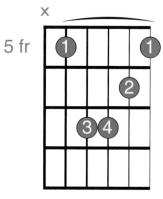
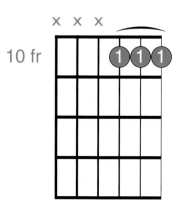

## Dm7

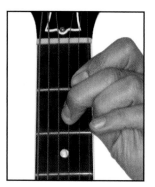
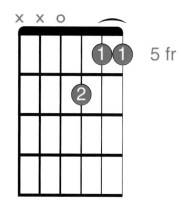

## D6

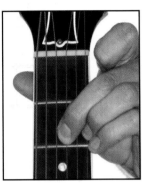
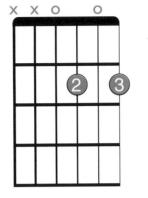
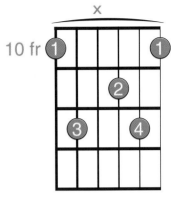

## Dm6

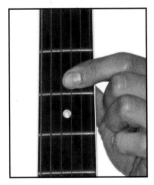
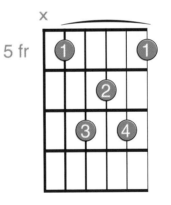

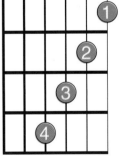

D

## D maj7

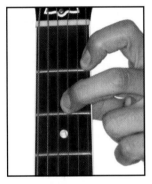
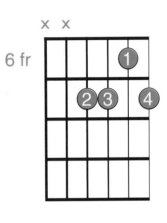
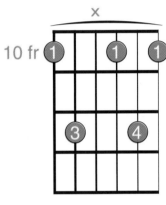

## D9

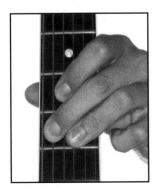
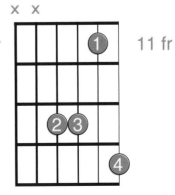
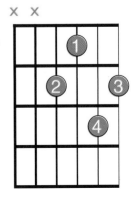

**D♯**

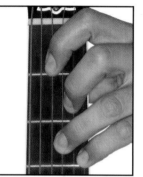

3 fr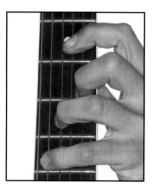

6 fr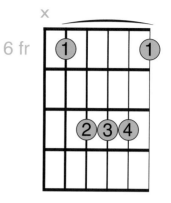

8 fr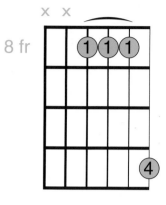

**D♯7**

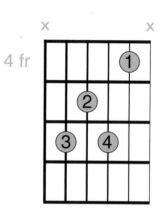

4 fr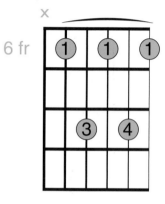

6 fr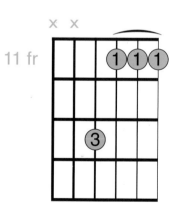

**D♯m**

3 fr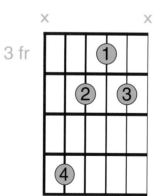

6 fr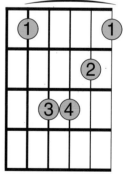

11 fr

**D♯m7**

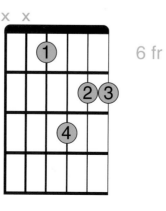

6 fr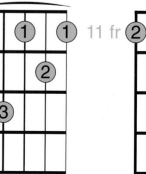

11 fr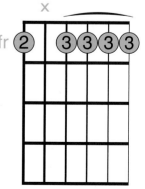

**D♯**

# KEY OF D♯/E♭

**D♯6**

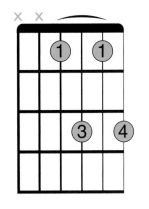 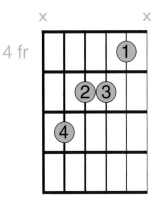 4 fr  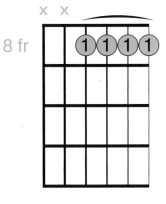 8 fr

**D♯m6**

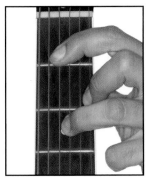

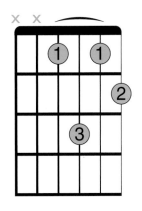 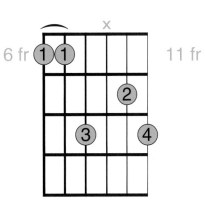 6 fr  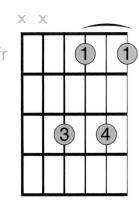 11 fr

**D♯ maj7**

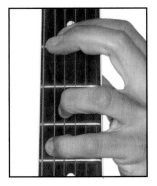

3 fr 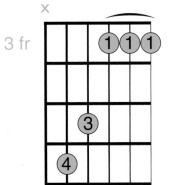 6 fr 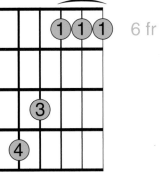 8 fr

**D♯9**

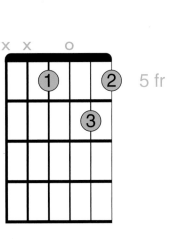 5 fr 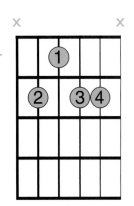 6 fr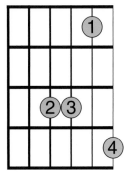

**D♯**

**19**

# KEY OF E

**E**

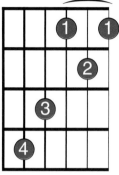

4 fr

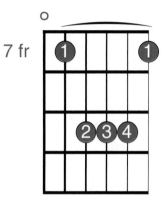

7 fr

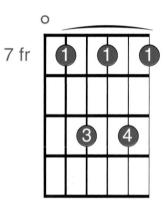

**E7**

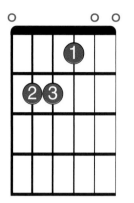

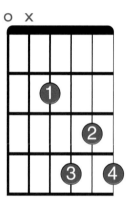

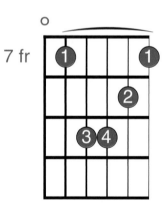

7 fr

**Em**

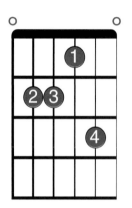

3 fr

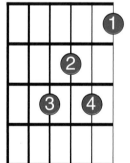

7 fr

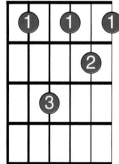

**Em7**

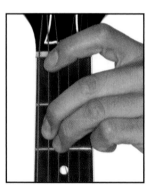

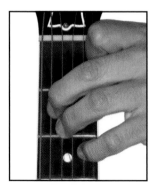

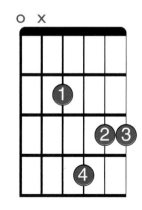

7 fr

## E6

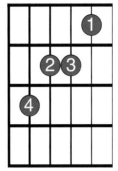

5 fr

9 fr

## Em6

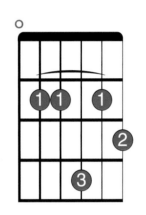

7 fr

## E maj7

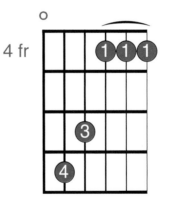

4 fr

7 fr

## E9

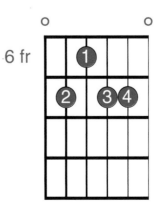

6 fr

7 fr

**E**

# KEY OF F

**F**

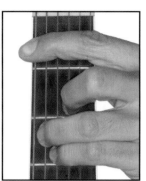

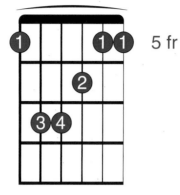

5 fr

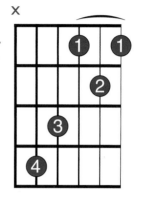

8 fr

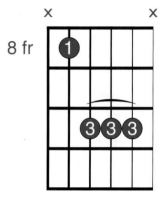

**F7**

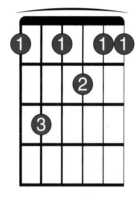

3 fr

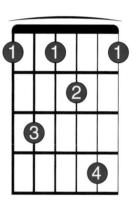

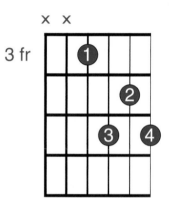

**Fm**

4 fr

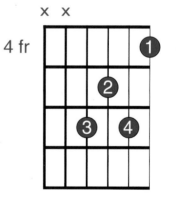

8 fr

**Fm7**

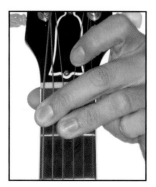

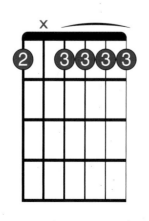

8 fr

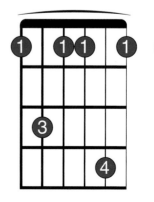

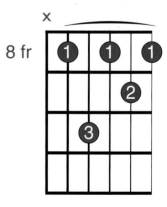

**F**

**F6**

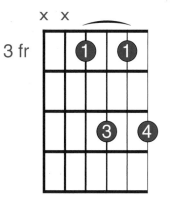

3 fr

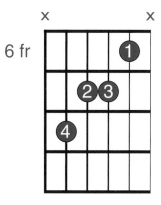

6 fr

**Fm6**

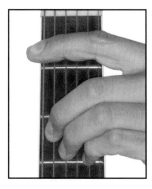

3 fr

8 fr

**F maj7**

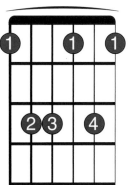

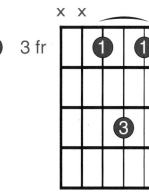

5 fr

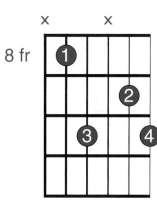

8 fr

**F9**

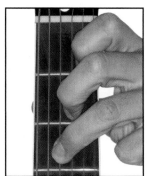

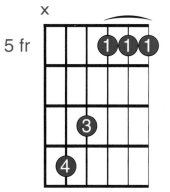

7 fr

8 fr

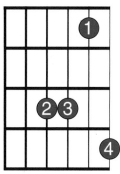

**F**

# KEY OF F#/G♭

**F#**

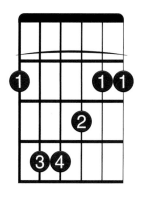

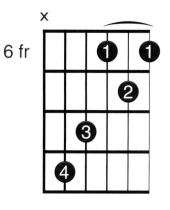 6 fr

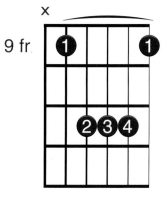 9 fr

**F#7**

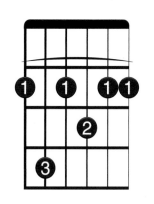

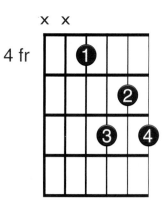 2 fr

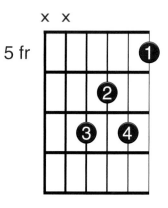 4 fr

**F#m**

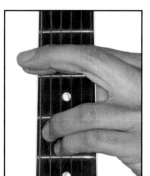

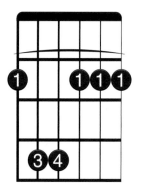

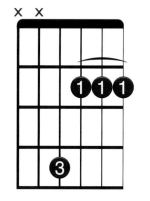 5 fr

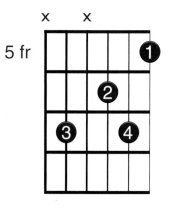

**F#m7**

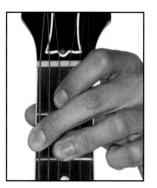

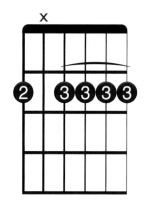

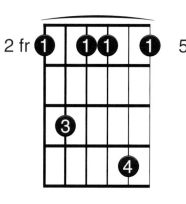 2 fr

5 fr

**F#**

24

# KEY OF F#/G♭

**F#6**

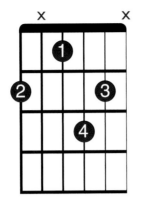

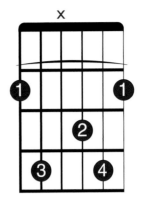

4 fr

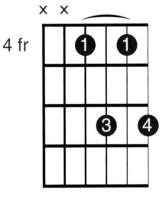

**F#m6**

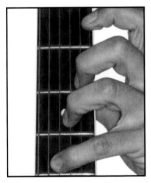

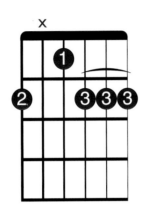

4 fr

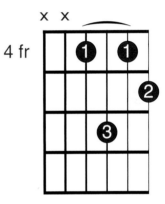

**F# maj7**

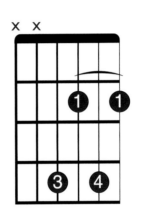

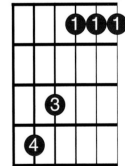

6 fr

**F#9**

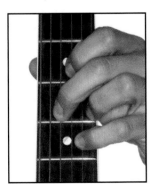

3 fr

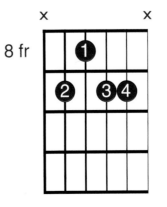

8 fr

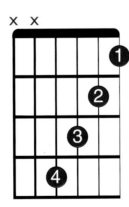

9 fr

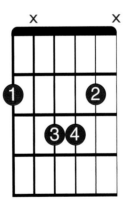

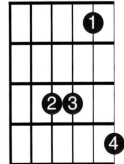

F#

# KEY OF G

**G**

3 fr

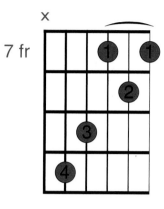

7 fr

**G7**

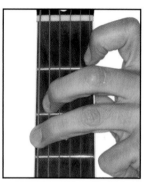

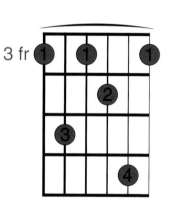

3 fr

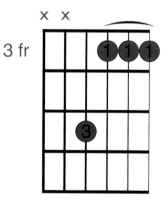

5 fr

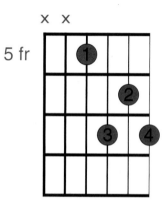

**Gm**

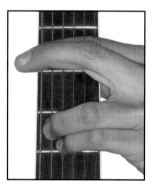

3 fr

3 fr

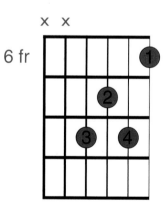

6 fr

**Gm7**

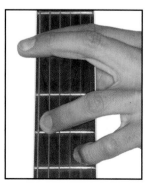

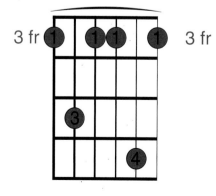

3 fr

3 fr

5 fr

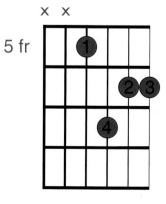

G

# KEY OF G

**G6**

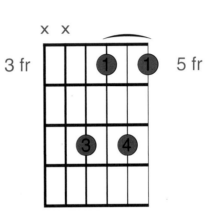

3 fr

5 fr

**Gm6**

x

3 fr

5 fr

**G maj7**

x x   2 fr

3 fr

7 fr

**G9**

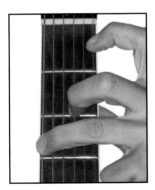

x o   o

4 fr

9 fr

**G♯**

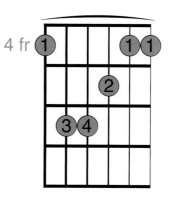
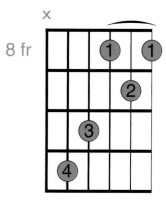

**G♯7**

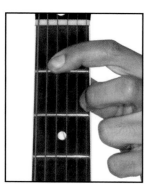
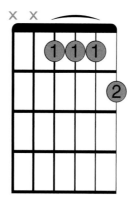
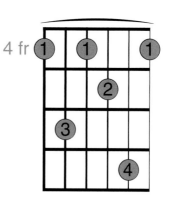
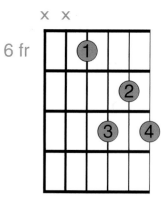

**G♯m**

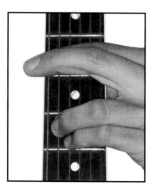
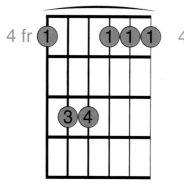
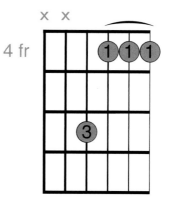
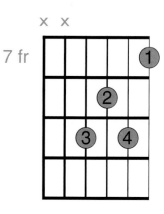

**G♯m7**

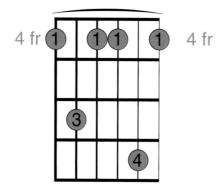
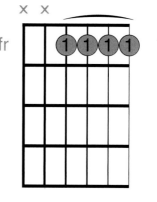
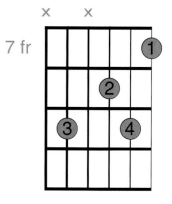

**G♯**

# KEY OF G♯/A♭

**G♯6**

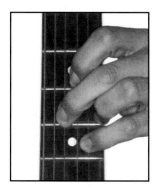

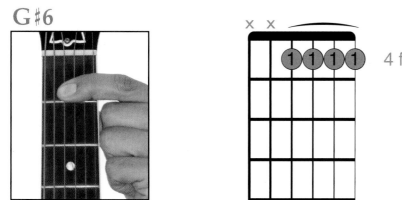

**G♯m6**

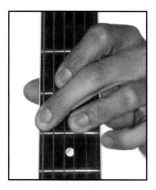

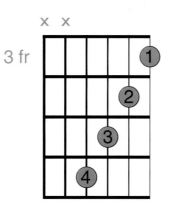 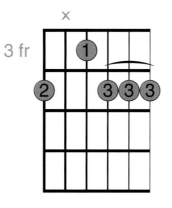

**G♯ maj7**

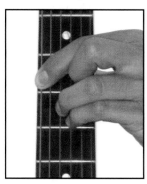

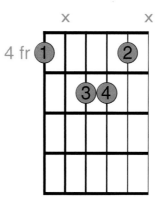 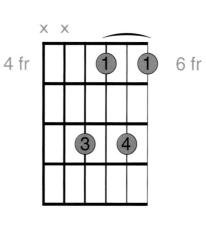 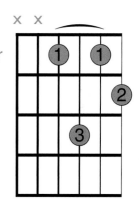

**G♯9**

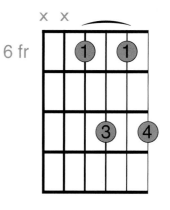

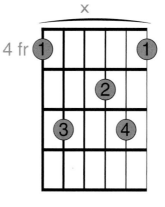 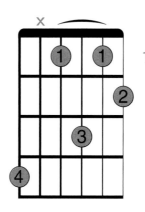 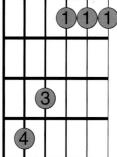

29

# DIMINISHED CHORDS

### A dim 7

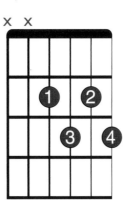

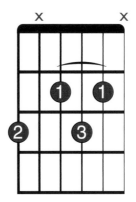

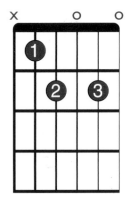

### E dim 7

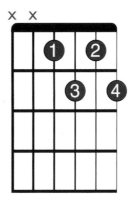

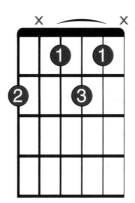

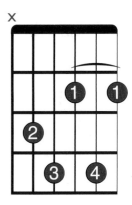

### F dim 7

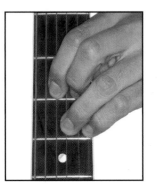

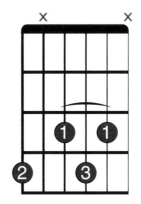

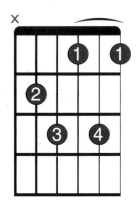

# AUGMENTED 7TH CHORDS

## C7 aug

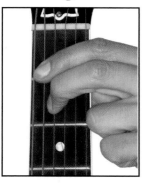

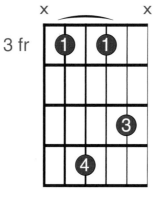

## F7 aug

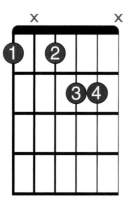

## D7 aug

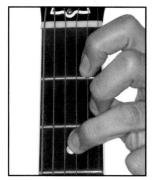

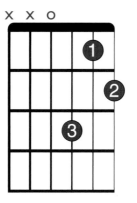

## G7 aug

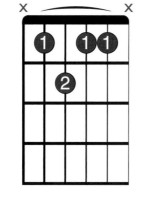

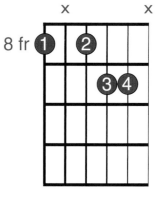

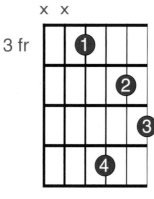

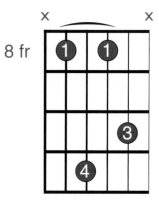

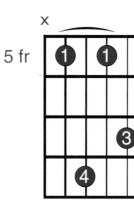

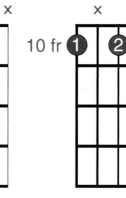

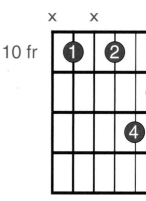

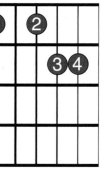

aug

# CHORD SEQUENCES – KEY OF A

The following chord progressions, to be used as exercises, are widely used and can be found in many songs. The chords have been grouped according to the eight most useful chords in each key, and are shown at the top of the page for easy reference. Any position of the chord can be used, however, and it would be excellent practice to substitute other positions of the chord when doing this exercise.

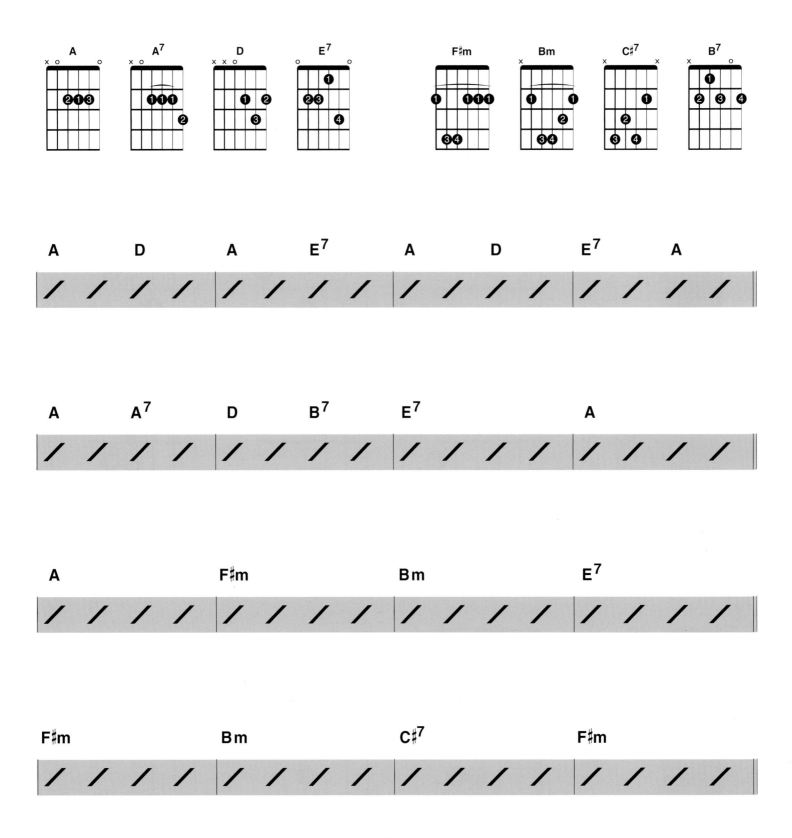

# CHORD SEQUENCES – KEY OF C

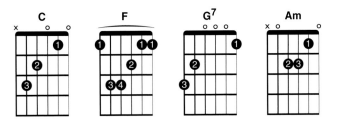

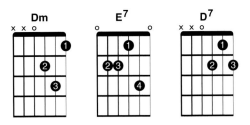

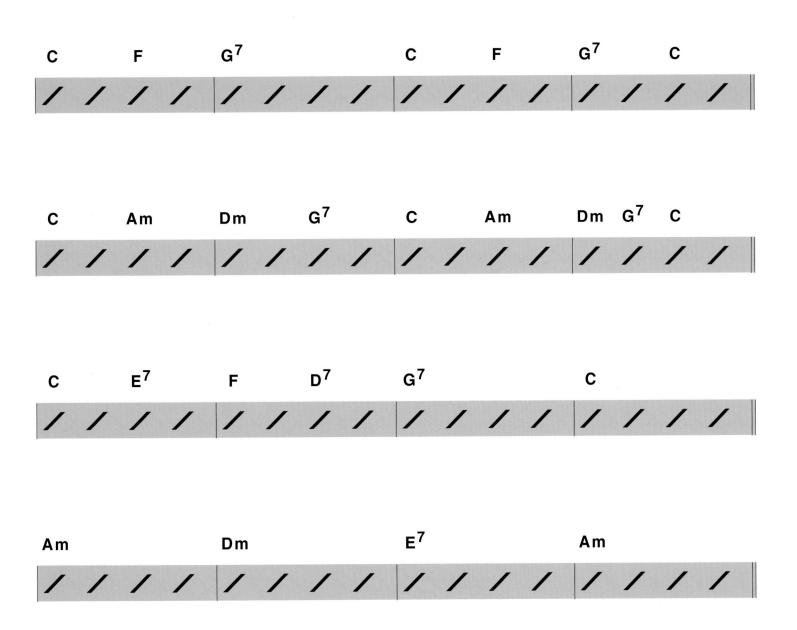

# CHORD SEQUENCES – KEY OF D

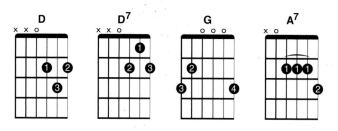

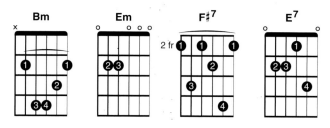

| D | D⁷ | G | D | A⁷ | D |
|---|----|---|---|----|---|

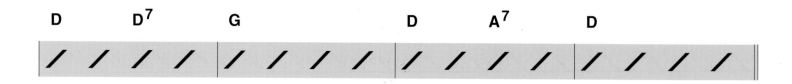

| D | Bm | G | A⁷ |
|---|----|---|----|

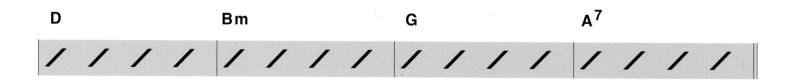

| D | F♯⁷ | G | E⁷ | A⁷ | D |
|---|-----|---|----|----|---|

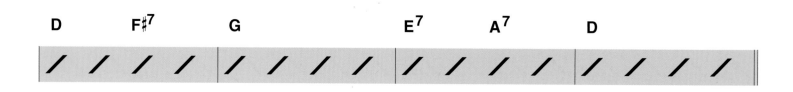

| Bm | F♯⁷ | Bm | Em | Bm | F♯⁷ | Bm |
|----|-----|----|----|----|-----|----|

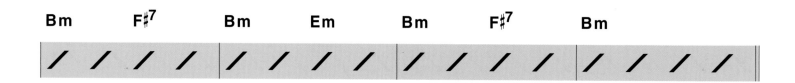

# CHORD SEQUENCES – KEY OF E

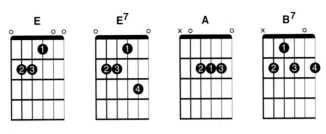

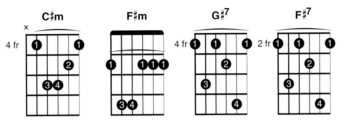

E      A      B⁷      A      E      A      B⁷      E

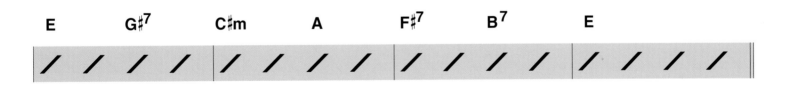

E      E⁷      A      F♯⁷      B⁷      E

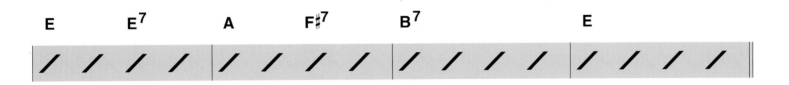

E      G♯⁷      C♯m      A      F♯⁷      B⁷      E

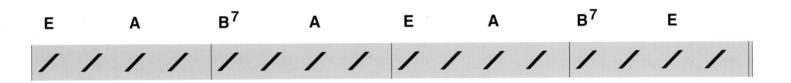

C♯m      F♯m      G♯⁷      C♯m

# CHORD SEQUENCES – KEY OF F

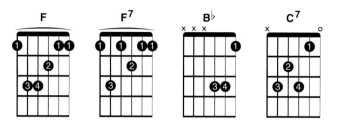

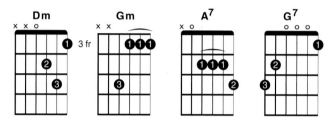

| F | | B♭ | | C⁷ | | | | F | | B♭ | | C⁷ | | F | |
|---|---|---|---|---|---|---|---|---|---|---|---|---|---|---|---|
| / | / | / | / | / | / | / | / | / | / | / | / | / | / | / | / |

| F | | Dm | | Gm | | C⁷ | | F | | Dm | | C⁷ | | F | |
|---|---|---|---|---|---|---|---|---|---|---|---|---|---|---|---|
| / | / | / | / | / | / | / | / | / | / | / | / | / | / | / | / |

| F | | A⁷ | | Dm | | G⁷ | | C⁷ | | B♭ | | F | | | |
|---|---|---|---|---|---|---|---|---|---|---|---|---|---|---|---|
| / | / | / | / | / | / | / | / | / | / | / | / | / | / | / | / |

| Dm | | Gm | | Dm | | A⁷ | | Dm | | Gm | | A⁷ | | Dm | |
|---|---|---|---|---|---|---|---|---|---|---|---|---|---|---|---|
| / | / | / | / | / | / | / | / | / | / | / | / | / | / | / | / |

# CHORD SEQUENCES – KEY OF G

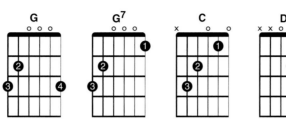

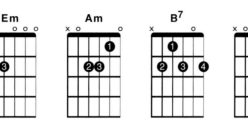

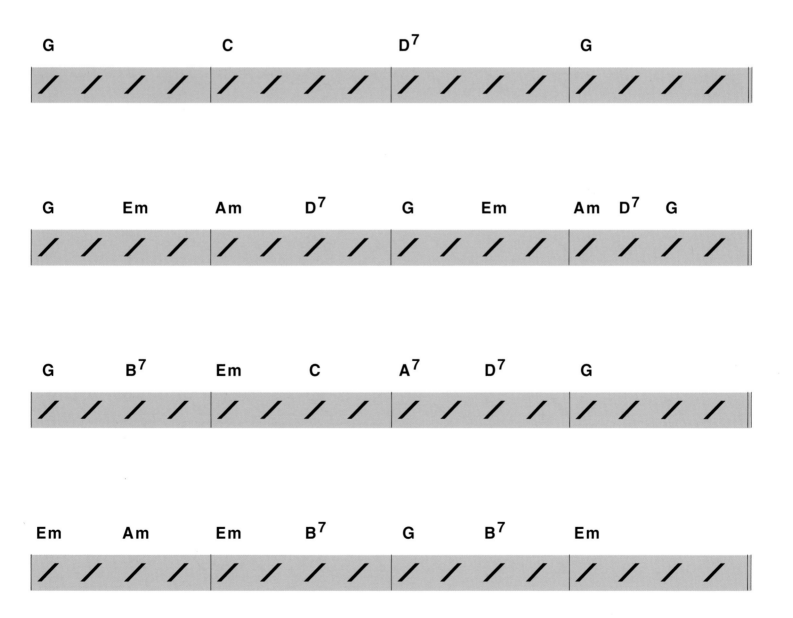

# 12-BAR BLUES SEQUENCE

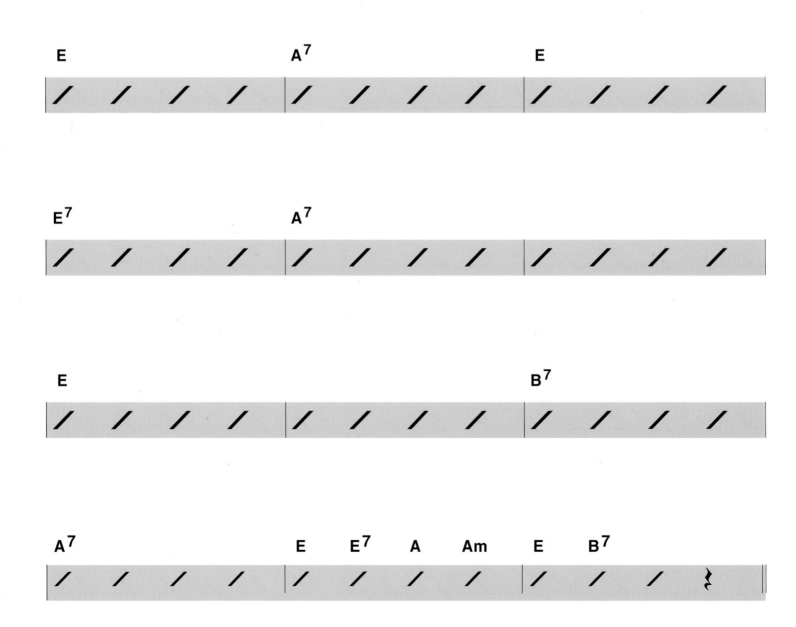

# DIXIELAND SEQUENCE

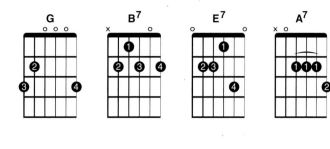

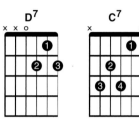

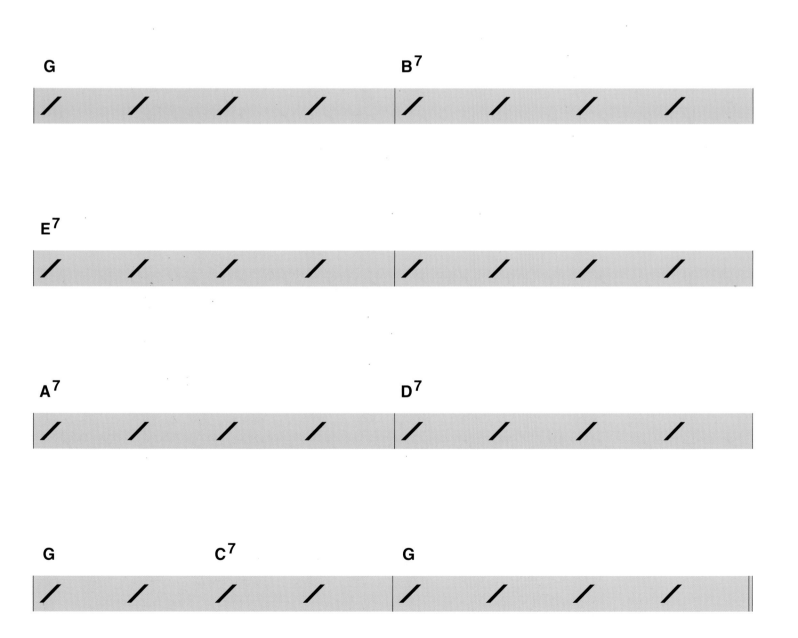

# ROCK 'N' ROLL SEQUENCE

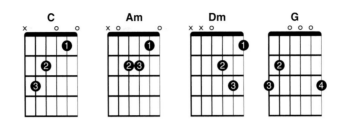

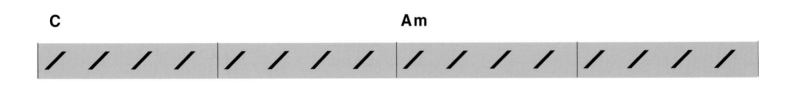

**C**                                          **Am**

**Dm**                                          **G**

**C**                                          **Am**

**Dm**                                          **G**